W9-BHL-641

# Orienteering

By Joanne Mattern

**Consultant:**
Jon Nash
Director of Media Relations
United States Orienteering Federation
Forest Park, Georgia

**Capstone**
*press*

Mankato, Minnesota

Capstone High-Interest Books are published by Capstone Press
151 Good Counsel Drive, P.O. Box 669, Mankato, Minnesota 56002
www.capstonepress.com

*Library of Congress Cataloging-in-Publication Data*
Mattern, Joanne, 1963–
    Orienteering / by Joanne Mattern.
    p. cm.— (Great outdoors)
    Summary: Introduces the sport of orienteering, in which competitors use
compasses and maps to navigate a racecourse, usually through the woods,
trying to find the best route and finish in the fastest time.
Includes bibliographical references and index.
    ISBN 0-7368-2411-1 (hardcover)
    1. Orienteering—Juvenile literature. [1. Orienteering.] I. Title.
II. Series.
GV200.4.M38 2004
796.58—dc22                                                    2003014556

**Editorial Credits**
James Anderson, editor; Timothy Halldin, series designer; Molly Nei,
    book designer and illustrator; Jo Miller, photo researcher

**Photo Credits**
Bruce Coleman, Inc./John P. Marechal, 43 (bottom); Lee Rentz, 42 (top); Norman
    Owen Tomalin, 43 (top)
Capstone Press/Gary Sundermeyer, cover (inset), 20
Corbis, cover (top)
Photri-Microstock/C.W. Biedel, 42 (bottom)
USDA/ARS/Scott Bauer, 38 (bottom)
U.S. Orienteering Federation/Andy Freeberg, 19; Greg Sack, cover (bottom), 10, 14, 27,
    36; Jerry and Marcy Monkman, 4, 24, 35, 41; Jerry Rhodes, 6, 9, 13, 17, 23, 32
Visuals Unlimited/Richard Walters, 38 (top)
**Capstone Press thanks Stephanie Martineau for her help in
preparing this book.**

1  2  3  4  5  6  09  08  07  06  05  04

# Table of Contents

# Orienteering

Throughout history, people have used maps and compasses for different activities. Explorers once followed a compass to get to distant lands. Pirates once used maps to lead them to buried treasure. Today, orienteering is a sport where competitors use maps and compasses to complete a race. Orienteering competitors are called orienteers.

During an orienteering event, each orienteer must reach several specific points on a planned racecourse. The goal is to find the best route to finish the course in the fastest time.

**Orienteers find points on a course marked by control flags.**

6

Orienteering events take place almost anywhere. Some events are held in parks or forests. Others are held in fields or on school grounds.

## The History of Orienteering

People have used maps and compasses to find their way for thousands of years. But the sport of orienteering is only about 100 years old.

In 1893, soldiers in Sweden and Norway were trained to use maps and compasses. In 1897, the first orienteering race was held in Oslo, Norway. The race tested the soldiers' mental and physical skills.

Soon, other people took part in the races. In Scandinavia, early orienteering races were held on skis. One race took place in a blizzard. This race covered 100 miles (160 kilometers) and took about 24 hours to finish.

**Orienteering events sometimes take place in open areas.**

After World War I (1914–1918), a Swedish man named Ernst Killander wanted more people to try track and field events. Killander organized races in fields and forests. He had each runner use a map and compass to follow the course.

## A Worldwide Sport

For many years, orienteering was only popular in Scandinavia. During the 1960s, it also became popular in other European countries. News of the sport spread to the United States and Canada.

People around the world now enjoy orienteering for several reasons. It is a fun way to get exercise. Orienteers spend time outdoors and enjoy nature. They also use reasoning and planning skills.

**Many orienteers enjoy the physical challenge that the sport offers.**

# CHAPTER 2

# Equipment

Orienteers need only a few items to enjoy their sport. These items include a map and compass. Comfortable clothes and shoes or hiking boots are also important.

## The Compass

The compass is one of the most important tools to orienteers. Any kind of compass can be used, but most orienteers use a base plate compass. These compasses are attached to a clear plastic base.

Some base plate compasses are designed especially for orienteering. They are easy to carry and use.

**Many orienteers wear T-shirts and jeans.**

## Topographical Maps

Topographical maps are another important orienteering tool. These maps show the elevation, or height, of the land. Topographical maps show streams, rocks, boulders, fences, and other landmarks and objects. Symbols on the map represent the location of these items.

Maps must be accurate and easy to read. Some orienteering maps are printed in color. Orienteers find these maps easy to read because similar symbols are the same color.

Orienteers carry the maps with them on the race. Sometimes maps are dropped or are damaged by rain or wind. Many competitors use a plastic envelope called a map case. This envelope protects maps from dirt and water.

## Control Sheets and Cards

A registration official gives each orienteer a control sheet before an event begins. This sheet of paper lists the start and finish points of the race. Symbols on the sheet describe each control point. The control sheet also shows the length and elevation of the course.

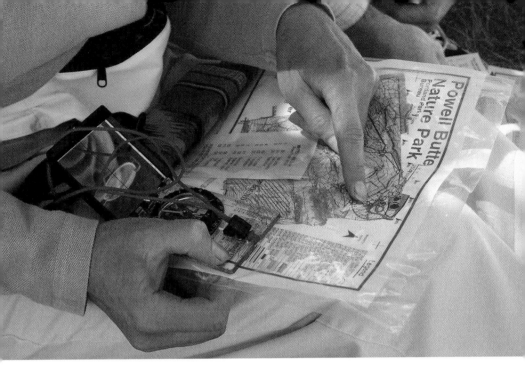

**Orienteers use topographical maps.**

The registration official also gives a control card to each orienteer. The card lists the orienteer's name and racing number. Boxes are printed on the card. One box must be punched at each control point. The competitor uses a needle punch located at each point to punch the boxes. Each punch makes a different pattern on the control card. The punch pattern at each control point tells officials which points were reached.

201

silva

14

At some events, orienteers use electronic clocks instead of control cards. Each orienteer fastens a piece of plastic to one finger. A computer chip is inside the plastic. When orienteers arrive at a control point, they hold the plastic piece near an electronic clock. The clock then records the orienteers' times.

Many orienteers like electronic clocks. They think that using the clocks is faster than using a punch. In the future, more orienteering events will use electronic clocks.

**Orienteers may use electronic clocks at some events.**

# Orienteering Officials' Duties

**Course Setters**
Design the course
Set control markers at proper locations

**Meet Directors**
Organize meet
Direct other officials

**Registration Officials**
Help orienteers sign up for the meet
Hand out maps and control cards

**Start Officials**
Control the start clock
Assign start times
Fill out orienteers' control cards
Give last minute instructions
Tell orienteers when to start

**Finish Officials**
Control the finish clock
Record finish times

**Results Officials**
Check punch patterns on control cards
Add orienteers' times and post results

17

## Clothing and Footwear

Orienteers wear clothes that keep them comfortable in the outdoors. Many competitors wear athletic pants and long-sleeved shirts. Others wear orienteering suits. Some wear jeans or shorts with a sweatshirt or T-shirt.

Orienteering suits are made of nylon or Lycra. These materials are stretchy and do not absorb moisture. Orienteering suits are made specifically for orienteers. Many of the suits are brightly colored.

Comfortable shoes are also important. Many orienteers wear running shoes or hiking boots. Orienteers need to wear shoes that are the correct size. Shoes that are too big or too small could cause blisters. Special orienteering shoes are also available. These shoes look like soccer shoes. They have rubber spikes on the soles. The spikes help orienteers get a good grip on rough terrain.

Some orienteers wear suits made of nylon or Lycra.

## Other Equipment

Orienteers use other items during an event. Some orienteers wear a pedometer. This device clips to a competitor's belt and counts the number of steps for them. This information helps orienteers tell how far they have gone. Some pedometers also measure an orienteer's speed and time.

control marker

needle punch

topographical map

jacket

control card

insect repellent

whistles

first aid kit

shoes

water bottle

watch

socks

pants

compass

## Equipment

- compass
- comfortable shoes and clothing
- control card
- control marker
- first aid kit
- insect repellent
- needle punch
- topographical map
- watch
- water bottle
- whistle

A good watch is an important piece of equipment for beginning orienteers. Watches help orienteers know how much time they have spent on the course. Any kind of watch can be used. Some orienteers like to wear stopwatches. Experienced orienteers often can tell how long a course will take just by looking at the map.

Some orienteers carry a magnifying glass with them. They use this device to view small features on the map. Orienteers can avoid mistakes when they see small features on a map.

Orienteers keep safety in mind. They carry a whistle. Each orienteer can use the whistle to call for help if someone is lost or injured.

First aid kits are available at all orienteering events. They are often found at the officials' table. Some orienteers carry small first aid supplies with them. Orienteers often run through the woods. Bandages are useful if an orienteer falls and scrapes the skin on a leg or elbow.

Orienteers need to drink plenty of water on the course. Lack of water can make orienteers sick. Many orienteers bring bottles of fresh water to drink along the course. Course organizers provide water at some events.

Some orienteers also bring small snacks with them on the course. Popular snacks are trail mix and granola bars.

Some events are held at night. Competitors in these events wear headlamps. Each orienteer wears a lamp. The lamps are held on their heads with an elastic band. The lamps allow competitors to keep their hands free to use the map and compass.

Other orienteering events take place on skis, on mountain bikes, on horses, and in canoes. These events require other equipment, such as warm clothes, helmets, or life jackets.

**Orienteering officials supplied water for this event.**

# CHAPTER 3

# Skills and Techniques

Orienteers use physical and mental abilities to complete an event. Physical fitness and map reading skills help competitors get better at the sport.

## Physical Fitness

Beginning orienteering events can be fun for any fitness level. First-time orienteers should start with short beginner courses. More experienced orienteers should match their level of fitness to the type of course. A person who exercises often will want the challenge of a longer or more difficult course.

Many orienteers enjoy the sport because it is a good way to get exercise.

Regular daily exercise can help orienteers improve their fitness level. They can get in shape by walking, running, or swimming.

## Mental Skill

Orienteering involves mental skill. Competitors make quick decisions based on information provided by the map and compass.

Course organizers do not give out the course map until just before the event begins. This rule makes sure that each orienteer has a fair chance to win an event.

Orienteers use the map to plan the best route. Sometimes the shortest route is not the best route. Running around a hill may be quicker or easier than climbing it. A shorter route may cover rough ground, while a longer route might have smooth ground. The smooth ground may be easier to run on and might allow an orienteer to take the lead in a race.

Orienteers must be willing to learn from their mistakes. If competitors make poor choices, they can use the information to make better decisions next time.

**Reading a map is a necessary skill in orienteering.**

## Map Skills

Map reading is the most important skill in orienteering. Each orienteer aligns their map soon after they receive it. They match features on their map to the features in the area.

To align a map, an orienteer looks for landmarks, such as a large rock or a tall tree. Each orienteer then finds this landmark on the

# Map Symbols

| | | | | |
|---|---|---|---|---|
| ━━━━━━ | paved road | | ── ──⟋ | fence: crossable, uncrossable |
| ▭ ▬ | pavement, gravel | | +──────+──────+ | powerline |
| ━━━━━ | dirt road | | ■ ∎ □ ✛ | building, ruin, tower |
| ── ── ── | vehicle track | | · • | boulder: small, large |
| ─────── | path | | △ | boulder group |
| ── ── ── ── | indistinct path | | ⦂⁖▲ ⁖⁖⁖ | boulder field, stony ground |
| ·─·─·─·─· | stone wall | | † × | cemetery, artifact |
| ⬬ ⬯ ᵥ | lake, pond, water hole | | ᴍᴍᴍ ᴍᴍᴍ | cliff: large, small |
| ∿∿∿ | stream: wide, narrow | | ⬬ ⊤ | bare rock, hunter's stand |
| ∿∿∿∿ | stream: intermittent, trickle | | ≈≈≈ | contour, index contour |
| ▤ | uncrossable marsh | | ∿ × ⋯ | form line, rootstock, ditch |
| ▤ | crossable marsh, wet ground | | · ᵥ ⌣ | dot knoll, pit, depression |
| ⟋∿⟍ ⬭ | distinct vegetation boundary | | +++++ ⬭ | earth dam, large depression |
| ▭ | slow run, walk, slow walk | | ▬ | open land |
| × ○ | trees: coniferous, deciduous | | ▭ ▦ | land: rough open, semi-open |
| ▥ | undergrowth: slow | | ▨ ▦ | felled area, sandy ground |
| ·-·-·-· | ruined stone wall | | | |

map. If the landmark is on the orienteer's left in the wilderness, it should also be on the left on the map. The orienteer then knows which way is north by matching north on the map to north on the compass. Aligning a map helps the orienteer travel in the right direction.

If no landmarks are available, orienteers align the map by using other details. They may look at changes in the trees or in a river they are following. They also look for changes in elevation, such as hills or drop-offs. If lines on a topographical map are close together, there is a hill in that area. Orienteers find hills and then match them with symbols on the map that show hills.

# Make Your Own Course

## What You Need:

blank pieces of paper
pencils, pens, or markers
5 pictures torn from a magazine
watch with a second hand or stopwatch

## What You Do:

1. Choose a place you would like to map. The area might be your backyard, a playground, or a school gym.
2. On your paper, draw the shape of the place you are mapping. If it is round, draw a circle. If it is a room in a school, it is probably shaped like a square or rectangle.

3. Draw all the things you see in the area. Try to draw them as close as you can on your map to where they are located in the area.
4. Look at your map one more time. Make sure you did not forget to draw any items from your area.

## You Have Just Made the Map:

Now you can set an orienteering course for your friends.

1. Look at your map. Decide where to put the control markers. The magazine pictures will be the control markers. Put a circle around each location, and number them starting with 1.
2. Leave a picture from a magazine at each location.
3. Invite your friends to go orienteering on your course. Instead of punching a control card at each control point, they should write down what they see in the magazine picture at each point. You can make it a race and time your friends to see who is fastest. Ask your friends what they wrote down about the pictures. See if they wrote similar descriptions.

# CHAPTER 4

# Responsible Orienteering

Orienteers use care when walking through the woods. They are careful not to injure themselves or damage the environment.

## Wilderness Trails

Orienteers should stay on trails as much as possible when walking through the wilderness. But some orienteering courses require orienteers to leave the trail.

People who leave the trail can crush plants under their feet. They can also damage the soil. Damaged soil washes away easily in the rain.

Many orienteering races for beginners take place on trails.

When orienteers leave a trail, they are careful not to damage any plants. They never pick flowers or plants.

Some orienteering courses may cross farmland or other private land. Course organizers get permission from the property owners before the event. Orienteers are careful not to damage or change property. They never move rocks or break fences or other objects.

## Keep It Clean

Orienteers care for the environment. They carry their trash out of the area.

Orienteers cut back on the amount of trash by carrying reusable items. They carry supplies in reusable bags. They carry water or sports drinks in plastic bottles.

**Orienteers who leave a trail are careful not to damage trees.**

# CHAPTER 5

# Safety

Orienteering events can cover rough ground. They may be held in harsh weather conditions. Orienteers must keep safety in mind at all times.

## Staying in Shape

Orienteering injuries may occur because competitors are not in good physical shape. These injuries could include muscle strains, sprains, or scrapes from falls. To help prevent injuries, orienteers stretch their muscles before beginning the course.

## Weather Safety

During warm weather, orienteers must stay cool. They wear comfortable clothes. They drink plenty of water. Orienteers wear sunscreen to protect their skin from the sun's rays.

Some orienteers carry basic first aid supplies in case they are injured on the course.

# Harmful Insects

## Mosquito

About 200 species of mosquitoes are found in the United States. Mosquitoes grow from eggs to adults in 14 days. Only female mosquitoes bite people and animals. Mosquito bites can develop into itchy bumps on a victim's skin. Mosquito bites can also carry diseases such as malaria and West Nile virus.

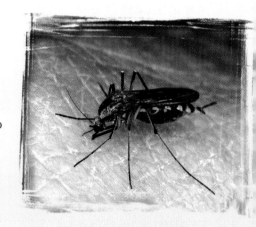

## Deer Tick

Deer ticks are found in wooded areas in the central United States and Canada. Deer ticks live about two years. During their life cycle, deer ticks feed only three times. Young ticks feed on small animals such as mice. Ticks develop a disease from the mice called Lyme disease. Lyme disease is dangerous to people.

Rain can make courses dangerous. Orienteers watch for slippery surfaces after a rainstorm. Rain can loosen rocks and dirt. Loose dirt and rocks can make a trail unsafe. Orienteers who get caught in a storm should seek shelter away from tall trees, cliffs, or water. Most events are canceled during thunderstorms.

## Insects

Insects can be a problem for orienteers. Mosquitoes can leave an itchy bite or even spread disease. To prevent mosquito bites, orienteers wear long-sleeved shirts and long pants. They also use insect repellent to keep bugs away.

The tick is another dangerous insect. These tiny, blood-sucking insects are common in parts of North America. Deer ticks can spread an illness called Lyme disease. Lyme disease can harm a person's heart and nervous system. Orienteers should check for ticks after being outside. Checking for ticks is the best way to prevent Lyme disease.

## Future of Orienteering

By following safety measures, orienteers keep the sport fun. Orienteering has become a popular family activity because it is fun for people of all ages.

Orienteering is gaining popularity. Many states or large cities have formed orienteering groups. More people join orienteering groups each year. These groups welcome new people to the sport of orienteering. The groups organize events that attract more people to the sport.

Some orienteers compete at state and national levels. Almost every country has national orienteering competitions. The winners of these competitions often compete in the World Orienteering Championships.

Racers who do well at local events can move on to the World Orienteering Championships.

41

# Poisonous Plants

## Poison Ivy

Poison ivy leaves grow in groups of three. The middle leaf is usually larger than the other two leaves. The plant often grows on tree trunks in wooded areas. Poison ivy is found in eastern and central North America. People who touch poison ivy often suffer from an itchy skin rash.

## Poison Oak

Poison oak grows as a bushy plant. The plant's leaves are covered with hairlike growth. Poison oak grows throughout the western and southeastern United States and in parts of Canada. Poison oak leaves are oval-shaped. Poison oak causes an itchy rash to develop when it comes in contact with a person's skin.

## Poison Sumac

Poison sumac is a shrub that grows green-white berries. The plant is green during the summer and turns yellow or red during the fall months. Poison sumac grows in wet, swampy areas in the southern and northern United States. Poison sumac's flowers produce an itchy oil that can get on people's skin and clothing.

## Stinging Nettle

Stinging nettle grows throughout the United States and Canada. Stinging nettle grows from a large main stem. Red-brown or green-white flowers grow from the plant's stem. Stinging nettle has dark green leaves. The plant's stem and leaves are covered with small hairs that irritate a person's skin.

# Glossary

**blister** (BLISS-tur)—a sore bubble of skin filled with liquid such as water or blood; blisters often are caused by something rubbing against the skin.

**compass** (KUHM-puhss)—an instrument people use to find the direction in which they are traveling; compasses have a needle that points north.

**landmark** (LAND-mark)—a familiar object that can be seen from far away

**pedometer** (peh-DAH-muh-tur)—a device that measures how far a person walks

**terrain** (tuh-RAYN)—ground or land

**topographical map** (tah-puh-GRAH-fih-kal MAP)—a map that shows the physical features of an area, including elevation, rivers, and landmarks

# Read More

**Bratt, Ian.** *Orienteering.* Mechanicsburg, Penn.: Stackpole Books, 2002.

**Sharth, Sharon.** *Way to Go! Finding Your Way with a Compass.* Reader's Digest Explorer Guides. Pleasantville, N.Y.: Reader's Digest Books, 2000.

# Useful Addresses

**The Canadian Orienteering Federation**
Box 62052
Convent Glen P.O.
Orleans, ON  K1C 7H8
Canada

**U.S. Orienteering Federation**
P.O. Box 1444
Forest Park, GA  30298-1444

# Internet Sites

FactHound offers a safe, fun way to find Internet sites related to this book. All of the sites on FactHound have been researched by our staff.

Here's how:

1. Visit *www.facthound.com*
2. Type in this special code **0736824111** for age-appropriate sites. Or enter a search word related to this book for a more general search.
3. Click on the **Fetch It** button.

FactHound will fetch the best sites for you!

# Index